## Introduction/Motivation

This paper contributes to the discussion of whether large banks are subject to adequate market discipline or enjoy a "too-big-to-fail" subsidy in credit markets as a result of perceptions of potential government support. During the most recent financial crisis and in several prior episodes, the U.S. and other governments have rescued large financial institutions to avoid the financial instability they feared would result from the failure of those firms. Market participants may continue to evaluate certain large financial institutions based on the belief that the government would provide support to those institutions in a crisis, as opposed to evaluating them on the basis of their stand-alone credit risk.

A number of previous studies have used market data to evaluate creditors' perceptions that a company is too big to fail. This paper uses credit default swap (CDS) data. Arguably, this is a more transparent metric of the credit spreads banks face than deposit costs (see Jacewitz and Pogach, 2013 or Bassett, 2014), which can have fees or other terms that complicate cross-bank comparisons, or bond spreads (Santos, 2013 and GAO, 2014), which often contain call provisions. In theory, if market participants deemed a large bank too big to fail, the bank's CDS spread would trade tighter than suggested by its fundamental credit risk. The bank would, as a result, experience lower CDS spreads than financial institutions market participants did not view as too big to fail.

Efforts to identify the possible impact of the too-big–to-fail perception on banks' borrowing costs face several challenges. Borrowing costs reflect idiosyncratic credit risk of individual banks and liquidity differences in firms' borrowings.

Volz et al. (2011) use CDS data from Bloomberg for an international sample of 91 banks, including U.S. banks, coupled with expected default frequencies from Moody's KMV (now Moody's Credit Edge) data to control for credit risk. Volz et al. control for liquidity differences using bid-ask spreads. They examine the impact of size, measured as market capitalization plus the book value of liabilities and data on total assets and find evidence consistent with a too-big-to-fail subsidy. Although

1

the authors consider multiple measures of size and data providers, they only consider asset size as a linear variable and do not examine asset-size thresholds. This paper, on the other hand, uses dummy variables at various asset size cut-offs and compares them with models using different asset size cut-offs (threshold effects), along with the dollar value of assets (continuous effects).

Ahmed et al. (2014) use CDS data from Markit (the same source for this paper's CDS data) for a sample of 20 U.S. banks, as well as U.S. firms from other industries, and control for credit risk using expected default frequencies from Moody's Credit Edge and for liquidity using Markit's CDS depth measure (one of three CDS liquidity measures rolled into the Markit liquidity score used in this paper). Markit compiles its CDS data from the single name reference entity of the CDS transaction and creates a liquidity rating based on factors detailed in the data section of this paper. The authors also make use of corporate bond data from the Trade Reporting and Compliance Engine (TRACE) reporting system of the Financial Industry Regulatory Authority to consider too-big-to-fail effects in the pricing of executed bond trades. For CDS and bonds, the authors consider size as a linear variable, i.e., the log of the asset size of a firm as opposed to evaluating whether an asset-size threshold effect exists.[1] Ahmed et al. offer economies of scale as an alternative explanation of why a firm's asset size affects its observed CDS spreads. Their argument is that larger firms are more profitable and consequently less likely to default. However, it could be argued that market participants' view of the benefits of economies of scale on profitability is already taken into account by Moody's Credit Edge, the credit control variable that Ahmed et al. use, since that variable incorporates measures of profitability and also makes use of stock price data (which presumably would "price-in" such economies of scale).

Previous papers on this subject have sought to measure time-variation in large banks' funding advantages or to quantify the value of the taxpayer subsidy. This paper takes a different approach. We

---

[1] Additionally, expected default frequency (EDF) has a nonlinear relationship with observed CDS spreads, making it difficult to draw economic significance from the model's coefficients. For example, industries with a low median EDF may have observed CDS spreads that are less affected by a small change in EDF when compared to industries with a higher median EDF. According to the paper, the mean EDF for banks in the sample is the fourth highest of the 14 industries considered.

seek to identify where a possible too-big-to-fail effect for banks may be most in evidence by testing alternative specifications of size and systemic importance. Specifically, we consider whether market participants allow firms to borrow at a lower cost based on various asset-size thresholds or whether those firms have been designated by the Basel Committee on Banking Supervision as globally systemically important banks (or G-SIBs).[2] We focus on asset-size thresholds and the G-SIB designation because regulators have used both types of measures to set heightened levels of prudential regulation. The paper approaches the analysis in two steps.

First, the paper tests two different alternative controls for credit risk before considering whether size appears to influence a bank's CDS spread. Each of the credit control variables is commonly used by market participants. Several papers use Moody's Credit Edge to control for credit risk (Volz et al., 2011 and Ahmed et al., 2014); other papers use controls for credit risk that reflect the authors' own perceptions of drivers of credit fundamentals (GAO, 2014). This paper selects the best fitting commercial credit model from two alternative models and then approaches the too-big-to-fail question.

With regards to controls for liquidity, papers use different control variables depending on the type of bank liability they are assessing. Papers considering deposits use deposit volumes while papers evaluating bond spreads use bid-ask spreads (GAO, Santos) to control for differences in liquidity across banks' liabilities. Other papers on CDS have used bid-ask spreads (Volz) or depth, i.e., the number of dealers quoting (Ahmed). This paper uses Markit's CDS liquidity score, which is a multifaceted measure that reflects: 1) the freshness of the quote, 2) depth of the market, and 3) the bid-ask spread. These refinements still yield results consistent with a number of other studies' findings that suggest a possible funding advantage for large banks.

The too-big-to-fail subsidy may be relevant to the policy discussion on appropriate asset-size thresholds for heightened prudential regulation. Since the financial crisis of 2007-09, large banks have

---

[2] See OFR Brief "Systemic Importance Indicators for 33 U.S. Bank Holding Companies: An Overview of Recent Data" for a discussion of the BCBS G-SIB methodology.

become subject to heightened prudential regulation and oversight both domestically and internationally. The Dodd-Frank Wall Street Reform and Consumer Protection Act introduced thresholds for prudential regulation for U.S. banks. Section 165 of the Act requires that "in order to prevent or mitigate risks to the financial stability of the United States," the Federal Reserve establish for all bank holding companies with at least $50 billion in assets prudential standards that "are more stringent" than generally applicable standards and that "increase in stringency" be based on a variety of factors related to the systemic importance of these institutions. Among other things, the Dodd-Frank Act also requires that banks with assets greater than $50 billion be subject to ex-post assessments in the event of taxpayer losses as a result of resolution of a firm under Title II of the Act. After the failures or near-failures of many large institutions during the financial crisis, legislation and regulation sought to make larger firms more safe and sound through heightened prudential standards, including higher capital and liquidity requirements. The higher standards attempt to ensure that these companies have sufficient capital and liquidity to weather a crisis, and they seek to promote market discipline by making it less likely that a large firm would need to be rescued. Under the Dodd-Frank Act, supervisory standards begin to increase at $50 billion in assets and become significantly more rigorous as companies become larger and more complex.

Based on analysis of market pricing, market participants appear to be offering cheaper funding to banks with assets above a certain threshold, which could encourage greater risk taking among these firms. We believe that this paper is unique in offering an analytic contribution to the policy discussion of the appropriate cut-off for heightened prudential regulation as it considers multiple asset-size thresholds and finds that using asset-size thresholds in the $50 billion to $150 billion range have the largest coefficients and best model fit for a too-big-to-fail effect. By contrast, models with asset-size thresholds at $200 billion or above are less effective at explaining banks' CDS spreads. Prior work in this area has considered too big to fail only as a linear function of bank size, but this paper explores too big to fail as a linear function and a threshold effect. We recognize that CDS spreads are but one way of measuring the too-big-to-fail subsidy and hope that this paper inspires further analytic work on where the too-big-to-fail threshold seems most material to better inform regulatory policy development. Although this paper contributes to the discussion of the appropriate cutoff for heightened prudential regulation of banks, evidence of a too-big-to-fail subsidy is only one of a number of relevant policy considerations. Other relevant considerations could include the data used in the Basel methodology for establishing the G-SIB systemic importance scores[3], continued rating agency ratings' uplift for some large U.S. banks, and how banks look on the basis of various cross sectional systemic risk measures, such as conditional value at risk or marginal expected shortfall.[4]

**Data**

*Sample*

The sample consists of 71 banks from North America, Asia, Europe, and Latin America. Twenty-one of these banks have been designated as G-SIBs by the Basel Committee. Banks were selected solely based on the availability of their pricing and transaction data in Markit and their financial data in the two commercial credit model providers we considered, Bloomberg and Moody's. Only publicly traded banks are represented in the sample, because the commercial credit models use a Merton type model to estimate default probability (distance to default) and then implied CDS spreads.[5] A Merton model views a bank's equity valuation as a call option on the total assets of the firm where the strike price is equal to its liabilities. These models can only to arrive at default estimates and implied CDS estimates for publicly traded banks.

The study compares different datasets on a monthly basis from April 2010 to March 2014. This period was chosen to examine the G-SIB variable as an indicator of too big to fail and to use Markit's

---

[3] See OFR Brief "Systemic Importance Indicators for 33 U.S. Bank Holding Companies: An Overview of Recent Data."

[4] See OFR working paper "A Survey of Systemic Risk Analytics" for a discussion of these metrics.

[5] None of the models use observed CDS spreads as an input to estimate implied CDS spreads.

liquidity score for single-name CDS, a metric that began in April 2010. However, not all of the raw data we used are reported monthly. For daily data, we used the first data point available for the month, since monthly data generally reflects the first day of the month. For data available only quarterly or biannually, such as asset size, we repeated the available data for each month in the reported period.

*Dependent Variable*

*Credit Default Swap Spread* (y) — These data were retrieved from Markit, are available at a daily frequency, and are based on a collection of transactions and dealer quotes for the reference entity. The CDS spreads in this study are based on the single name reference entity of the CDS transaction. The data are recorded in percentages, so a regression coefficient of 1.30 represents 1.30 percent, or 130 bps. Five-year CDS spread data was chosen because it is the most liquid of the spread tenors and contains the most robust data. The CDS contracts are all quoted in U.S. dollars to avoid exchange rate challenges. Additionally, only spreads on senior CDS were used in this study. Lastly, restructuring clauses were streamlined by using the prevailing standards established by each country's regulatory regime. Variation in restructuring clauses is controlled for in the models through right-hand geographic variables. Each of these restrictions on the data set is meant to reduce the noisiness of the data and isolate the possible too-big-to-fail variables this paper is interested in investigating.

*Independent Variables*

*G-SIB(0,1), G-SIB(cap add-on)* — The global systemically important bank (G-SIB) designation is a label given by the Financial Stability Board (FSB). Established by the 2009 G-20 summit, the FSB has been tasked with monitoring the global financial system. The purpose of the G-SIB designation is to increase oversight of banks deemed systemically important and to provide a transparent, rules-based approach to determining higher capital adequacy requirements for these firms as part of Basel III. The first official

G-SIB list was published in November 2011,[6] but there were a number of leaks before that date including a leak to the *Financial Times* in November 2009.[7] To control for leaks of information, we decided to use the most recent iteration of the G-SIB list from November 2013 and apply it to the entire sample ranging back to April 2010. The G-SIB(0,1) variable is a binary indication of G-SIB designation, while the G-SIB(cap add-on) variable contains data points ranging from 0 to 250 basis points depending on which G-SIB risk-based capital add-on bucket the entity falls into. The larger the bucket, the greater the level of required additional capital with G-SIB(cap add-on) with values of 1 representing an additional 100 basis point requirement for banks' risk-based capital ratios and values of 4 being representing an additional 250 basis point requirement for banks' risk-based capital ratios.

*Assets > $50B … Assets > $250B* — These asset labels were assigned to explore potential too-big-to-fail threshold effects. They are binary dummy variables, for example, the "Assets > $50B" assigns a 0 for all banks with assets equal or less than $50 billion and a 1 to all banks with assets greater than $50 billion. Data on total assets was gathered from Bloomberg and, for non-U.S. institutions, converted into U.S. dollars using that period's exchange rate.

*Liquidity Fixed Effects* — Markit places a liquidity score on individual CDS contracts on a one-to-five scale, one being the most liquid. The liquidity score is assigned based on three factors: bid-ask spread, market depth, and data freshness. Each category has a number of demerits that raise the liquidity score of the entity. Factor 1 is bid-ask spread with a maximum of five demerits. The tightest bid-ask spreads have no demerits while the widest spreads have five demerits. Factor 2 is market depth with a maximum of four demerits. According to Markit, "[d]epth can refer to the number of dealers who are marking their books in Markit's end-of day service or those that are actively sending runs, combined

---

[6] See www.financialstabilityboard.org/publications/r_111104bb.pdf

[7] See www.ft.com/cms/s/0/df7c3f24-dd19-11de-ad60-00144feabdc0.html#axzz3EGCJrZ9E

with the volume of runs being sent. The higher the number of participants quoting or submitting end of day levels, the more liquid the entity-tier is likely to be." The final factor, factor 3, is data freshness with a maximum of two demerits. To calculate demerits, Markit uses a basic equation that takes into account the time individual contributor prices were last updated. A dummy liquidity score of one to five is then produced based on the total number of demerits.[8] Because liquidity is determined from a demerit system, it is run as a fixed effect with five different binary liquidity variables using a liquidity score of five as the base liquidity in the regressions. If a single liquidity variable is significant at the 90 percent confidence level, then the liquidity effects variable is marked "Yes."

*Geographical Fixed Effects* — This consists of binary dummy variables used to control for geopolitical factors that could potentially influence CDS spreads. For the purposes of this study, North America is the reference geographical zone. Because of data and sample size restrictions, there are no banks included from Africa or the Middle East.

*Time Fixed Effects* — These are a collection of dummy variables meant to control for potential time-varying risk aversion that could exert a systemic influence on observed CDS spreads. The data covers a period from April 2010 to March 2014, and each of these years is introduced as a binary variable. If one of the time variables is statistically significant at the 90 percent confidence level, then time fixed effects are reported as a "Yes" in the regression results.

*Bloomberg five-year estimated CDS spread* — This variable is derived from the Bloomberg "DRSK model" available via the Bloomberg terminal. At its core, the DRSK model uses a Merton methodology to

---

[8] The exact ranges and calculations of demerits and the final liquidity score calculation can be found in the Markit user manual, accessible to subscribers of the database.

estimate distance to default and derive estimated CDS spreads from data on a firm's balance sheet, share price, and share price volatility. Additional adjustments are made to the classic Merton model to adapt it to estimating CDS spread. More details can be found in a white paper available to Bloomberg terminal subscribers.[9]

*Moody's Credit Edge five-year estimated CDS spread* – This variable was obtained from Moody's Credit Edge service. It makes use of Moody's enriched Merton model that considers market-based measures of leverage and asset volatility in estimating a firm's CDS spread.

**Part 1: Evaluation of Fundamental Models**

**Table 1.1: Part 1 Summary Statistics — Total Sample Size = 38**

| | No. of Banks | Req. Capital Add-Ons | Max Asset Size | Median Asset Size | Min Asset Size | Max CDS Spread | Median CDS Spread | Min CDS Spread |
|---|---|---|---|---|---|---|---|---|
| Non-G-SIB | 23 | 0 bps | $934.9 B | $174.8 B | $36.3 B | 2,525 bps | 129 bps | 28 bps |
| G-SIB 1 & 2 buckets | 12 | 100 to 150 bps | $2,467.6 B | $1,123.7 B | $73.3 B | 592 bps | 139 bps | 37 bps |
| G-SIB 3 & 4 buckets | 3 | 200 to 250 bps | $2,585.3 B | $2,269.3 B | $1,864.7 B | 348 bps | 118 bps | 59 bps |
| Total | 38 | N/A | $2,585.3 B | $339.9 B | $36.3 B | 2,525 bps | 131 bps | 28 bps |

*Sources: Basel Committee on Banking Supervision and authors' calculations*

The table above outlines some summary statistics for the first part of this analysis. Bank of Nova Scotia, Bank of NY Mellon, and Wells Fargo rank among the lowest CDS spreads in the sample. The sample represents a broad range of bank sizes, from asset size of $36 billion to $2.6 trillion. To do a side-by-side comparison of the fit of the two credit models, we required that data for a given bank must be in

_____

[9] See Bloomberg, 2014.

the Markit, Bloomberg, and Moody's databases to be included in the regression in this part of the analysis. A consequence, however, is a more restricted sample of 38 banks compared to the 71 banks in part 2 of this paper.

The first test for heteroskedasticity used, the Breusch-Pagan Heteroskedasticity Test, indicated there was a presence of heteroskedasticity at the 99 percent confidence level. A further investigation, using the White test with Cameron and Trivedi decompositions, indicated the presence of skewness and kurtosis in the model at the 99 percent confidence level. For this reason, a standard "ordinary least squares," or OLS, regression would not give accurate results. A number of other papers in this literature make use of standard OLS.

In this section of the paper, two separate methods are used to overcome heteroskedasticity. The first method adds a robust option to the initial regression. The robust option chosen uses Huber-White sandwich estimators to estimate standard errors. This is commonly used as a minor correction for heteroskedasticity by producing estimators for ordinary data using stratified cluster sampling. The results of the robust regression follow in table 1.2. The regressions were reestimated clustering the banks by name to check for the presence of auto-correlation. These results are shown in Appendix A and do not alter the conclusions presented in the main text.

**Table 1.2: Robust OLS Fundamental Model Comparison**

| Dependent Variable:<br>**Markit Five-year CDS** | Baseline specification | Bloomberg | Moody's |
|---|---|---|---|
| Bloomberg five-year estimated CDS spread | | 0.879*** | |
| | | -0.0334 | |
| Moody's Credit Edge five-year estimated CDS spread | | | 0.963*** |
| | | | -0.0480 |
| Constant | 0.335*** | 0.313*** | -0.348*** |
| | -0.1350 | -0.0696 | -0.1190 |
| | | | |
| Liquidity Fixed Effects | Yes | Yes | Yes |
| Time Fixed Effects | Yes | No | Yes |
| Geographical Fixed Effects | Yes | No | Yes |
| | | | |
| Observations | 1,475 | 1,475 | 1,475 |
| R-squared | 0.170 | 0.918 | 0.696 |

*** p<0.01, ** p<0.05, * p<0.1

The time and geographical controls vary in significance as the right-hand-side variables are adjusted while the liquidity control remains constant throughout each regression. Bloomberg and Moody's are each significant at the 99 percent level when the basic set of controls is applied. To reveal which model has the most explanatory power, R-squared is used. In this model, Bloomberg has the most explanatory power with an R-squared of 91.8 percent while Moody's has an R-squared of 69.6 percent. Following is a scatterplot of the relationship between the Markit five-year CDS spread and Bloomberg's five-year estimated CDS spread.

**Graph 1.1: Bloomberg Five-year Estimated CDS Spread vs. Markit Five-year CDS Spread**

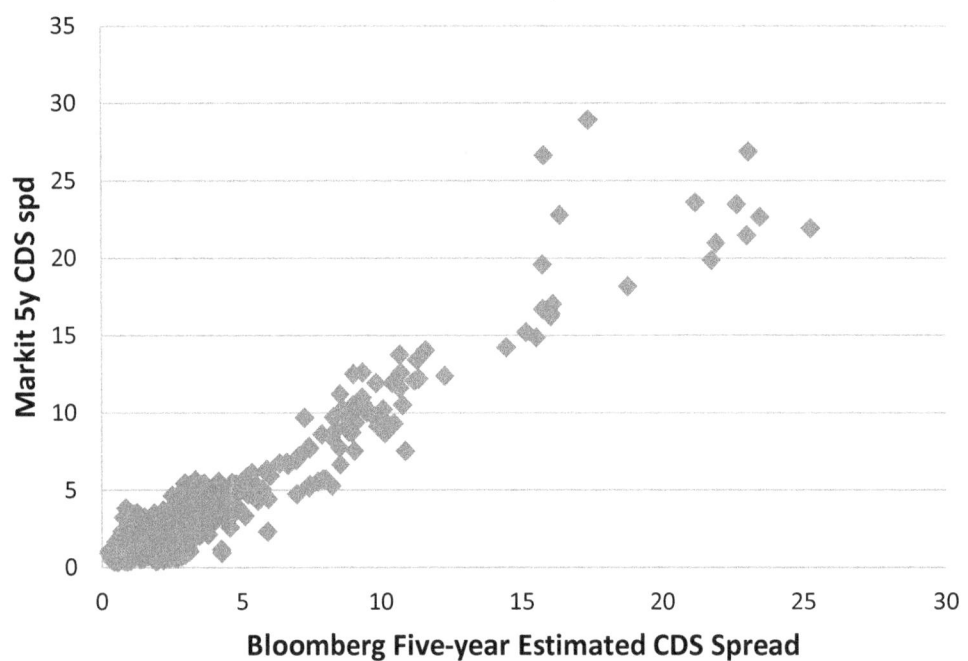

Graph 1.1 shows there is a clear positive relationship between the Markit five-year CDS spread and Bloomberg's five-year estimated CDS spread. This is consistent with the results of the robust OLS regression shown in table 1.2. The scatterplot also lends evidence toward a heavy and predictable skewness in the model. For this reason, along with the results of the Breusch-Pagan and White tests, a generalized least squares regression with a heteroskedastic correction option was used in addition to the robust OLS regression for this section of the paper. Table 1.3 shows the results of the GLS regression.

**Table 1.3: GLS Fundamental Credit Model Comparison**

| Dependent Variable: **Markit Five-year CDS** | Baseline specification | Bloomberg | Moody's |
|---|---|---|---|
| Bloomberg five-year estimated CDS spread | | 0.850*** | |
| | | -0.0115 | |
| Moody's Credit Edge five-year estimated CDS spread | | | 0. 734*** |
| | | | -0.0204 |
| Constant | 0.989*** | 0.273*** | 0.058 |
| | -0.0818 | -0.0383 | -0.0627 |
| | | | |
| Liquidity Fixed Effects | Yes | Yes | Yes |
| Time Fixed Effects | Yes | Yes | Yes |
| Geographical Fixed Effects | Yes | Yes | Yes |
| | | | |
| Observations | 1,475 | 1,475 | 1,475 |
| Bayesian Information Criterion | 6,895 | 3,479 | 5,419 |

*** $p<0.01$, ** $p<0.05$, * $p<0.1$

Bloomberg and Moody's are each significant at the 99 percent level when the basic set of controls is applied. To reveal which variable has the most explanatory power in this model, Bayesian Information Criterion (BIC) is used. BIC uses a likelihood function to determine the strength of a model. Lower BIC scores indicate a better fit model. To reach a BIC score within the GLS framework, the heteroskedasticity correction needed to be relaxed and the standard GLS autocorrelation model needed to be used. The BIC results of the robust OLS regression reinforce the finding that the model using Bloomberg's implied CDS spreads has the best fit.

The following graphs visually compare the models over time for two large U.S. banks. The charts illustrate the results of the GLS regression. The Bloomberg model, for the most part, appears to follow observed CDS spreads more closely than the Moody's model. For these reasons, the Bloomberg model is selected as the fundamental credit control, along with other controls, for the next phase of the analysis.

13

**Graph 1.2. Bank of America Five-year CDS Spread vs. Estimated CDS Spread Under Different Credit Models**

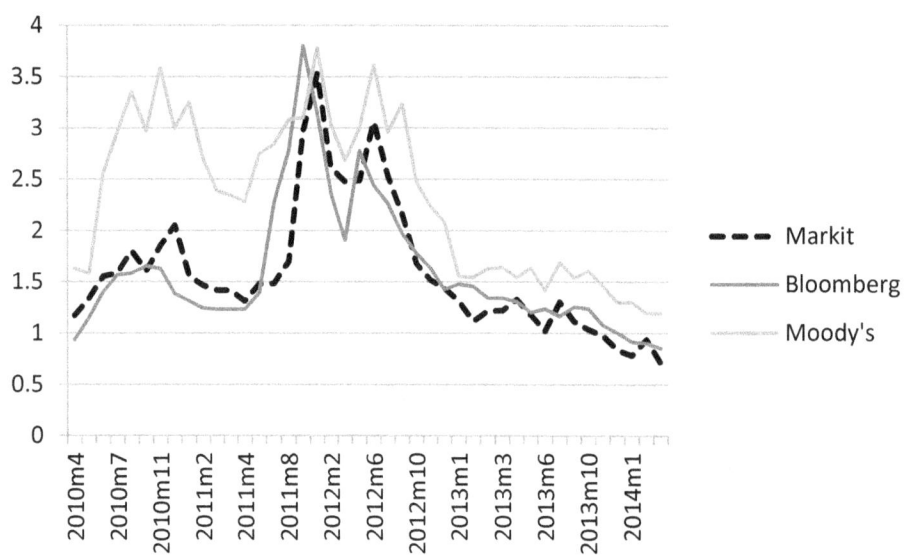

**Graph 1.3 Citigroup's Five-year CDS Spread vs. Estimated CDS Spread Under Different Credit Models**

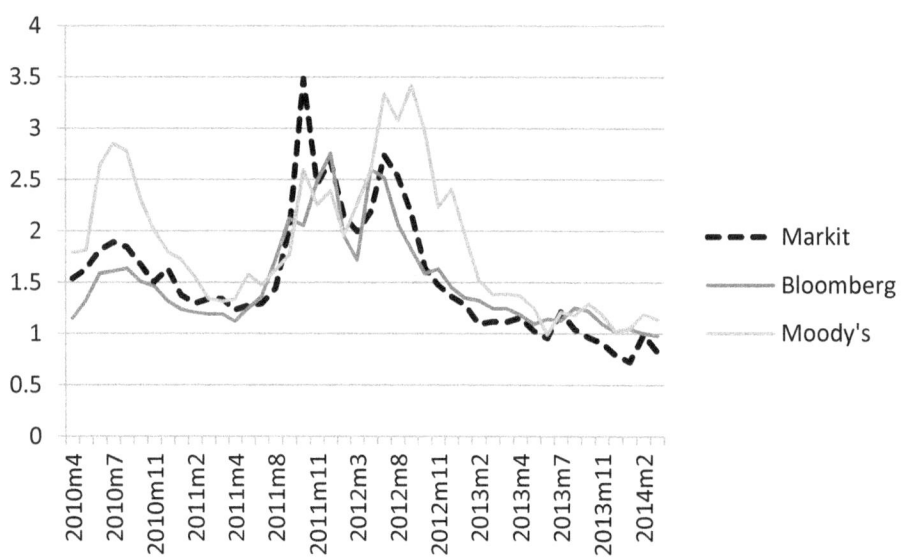

**Part 2: Evaluation of Too-Big-to-Fail Indicators**

In the previous analysis, the GLS and robust OLS models with Bloomberg had the most explanatory power. Additionally, the Bloomberg CDS spread variable was found to be statistically significant at the 99 percent confidence level in the previous model. For these reasons, Bloomberg's model CDS spread variable was applied for part 2 of this paper.

The next model in this study attempts to uncover which, if any, too-big-to-fail variable improves the model's predictive power for observed five-year CDS spreads. The variables being evaluated are asset thresholds of $50 billion to $250 billion, asset size as a linear variable, two alternative measures of G-SIB designation (G-SIB(0,1) and G-SIB(cap add-on), described previously) and clearing bank as a dummy variable. The sample increases, including a total of 71 banks for which both Markit and Bloomberg data are available. For this reason, the descriptive statistics on the sample change, with minimum asset size of $7 billion and maximum asset size of $4.6 trillion equivalent.

**Table 2.1: Part 2 Summary Statistics (U.S. dollars for asset size and percentage for CDS spread) — Sample Size = 71**

| | No. of Banks | Required RWA Capital Add-Ons | Max Asset Size | Median Asset Size | Min Asset Size | Max CDS Spread | Median CDS Spread | Min CDS Spread |
|---|---|---|---|---|---|---|---|---|
| Non-G-SIB | 50 | 0 bps | $1,975.3 B | $165.7 B | $6.8 B | 2,602 bps | 157 bps | 28 bps |
| G-SIB 1 & 2 Buckets | 16 | 100 to 150 bps | $3,174.3 B | $1,244.3 B | $73.3 B | 592 bps | 145 bps | 37 bps |
| G-SIB 3 & 4 Buckets | 5 | 200 to 250 bps | $4,596.1 B | $2,406.1 B | $1,864.7 B | 348 bps | 115 bps | 59 bps |
| Total | 71 | N/A | $4,596.1 B | $292.4 B | $6.8 B | 2,602 bps | 148 bps | 28 bps |
| Sources: Basel Committee on Banking Supervision and authors' calculations | | | | | | | | |

Graph 2.1, below, shows the distribution of banks based on the asset-size thresholds used in the part 2 analysis. The chart shows reasonably large shifts in distributions for most thresholds, except for the $125 billion and $150 billion thresholds. The small shift between the $125 billion and $150 billion asset thresholds (only one bank) provides some insight about why the results of the regression analysis for these two models were so similar (see tables 3.1 and 3.2).

**Graph 2.1: Bank Counts Grouped by Asset Size (U.S. dollars) (March 2014)**

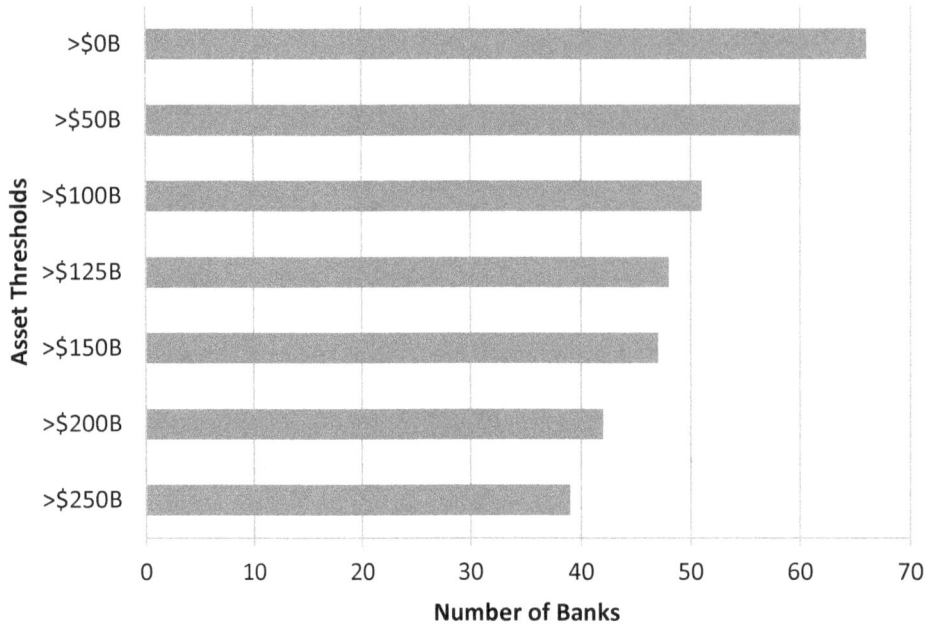

Tables 3.1 and 3.2 illustrate that, even when using the best credit and liquidity controls available, a model of banks' observed five-year CDS spreads is improved by using controls for a possible too-big-to-fail effect. We consider sequentially nine different possible too-big-to-fail control variables and each of them is significant at the 99 percent confidence level. The effect persists through different too-big-to-fail specifications, including the two G-SIB variables described previously, a linear asset size variable, various asset-size threshold variables, and a clearing bank dummy variable. In every instance, the too-big-to-fail coefficient is negative, indicating that greater size, being a G-SIB, or being a clearing bank results in lower observed five-year senior CDS spreads. This is broadly consistent with previous findings.

Although G-SIB includes asset size, it also reflects other factors, such as interconnectedness. One might imagine that as a multifaceted measure of systemic importance, it could better capture potential too-big-to-fail effects. However, when comparing G-SIB variables to the asset size variables, asset size has substantially greater descriptive power and economic significance than a bank's G-SIB status. For example, the coefficient on G-SIB (0,1) is only -15 basis points and the improvement in the BIC is minimal relative to alternative models that use asset-size thresholds.

When looking at asset size, it appears as if the too-big-to-fail effect is more akin to a threshold effect than linear. The BIC is lower for nearly every size asset-threshold variable when compared to the linear size asset variable; which indicates greater descriptive power. Among the asset-size thresholds, the model suggests that the $50 billion asset threshold is the most economically significant (highest coefficient) cutoff while the $150 asset threshold is the most statistically significant (lowest BIC). [10] According to this model, banks with assets in excess of $50 billion on average experience a 80 basis point decline in their CDS spread when controlling for credit fundamentals, liquidity of the CDS and other factors.[11] The $150 billion threshold is significant at the 99 percent level and has the greatest descriptive power. It should be noted that the $50 billion and $150 billion thresholds have similar coefficients, while the $125 billion and $150 billion thresholds have similar BICs. The similarity in results for the $125 billion and $150 billion thresholds is not surprising given the lack of variation in the sample (depicted in graph 2.1).

Relative to a model with no too-big-to-fail variables, the BIC falls from 9,087 to 8,740 in the model with the inclusion of the $150 billion threshold (Table 3.1). This implies a substantial improvement in the model's performance as a result of the inclusion of this asset-size threshold. The probability of the original specification being as strong as the specification including the $150 billion threshold variable is nearly zero (less than 0.0000001 percent). The inclusion of an additional dummy variable for clearing banks (shown in Table 3.2) adjusts the economic significance of the asset-variable size slightly, but otherwise maintains the conclusion of Table 3.1. It marginally improves the BIC of the

---

[10] Specifically, the BIC equals -2 * log-likelihood + (# of parameters) x (penalty that depends on the number of data points). When two models have the same number of data points and parameters, the second term will be identical across all models, and so the only difference is -2 * log-likelihood. So half of the BIC difference measures the log-likelihood difference between models, and in a pseudo-Bayesian interpretation the odds of one model being no different than the other, is approximately exp ((BIC_1 − BIC_2)/2). So, the BIC for the asset-size threshold model relative to the log-asset-size model indicates a much better fit of the asset-size threshold model.

regression as well. The robust regression in Appendix B checks for autocorrelation in the same fashion as the previous section of this paper, by clustering based on bank name. Ideally, the model would be checked using first differences. However, in the sample, bank size is highly persistent and so there is little time series variation in bank size to identify this effect. In the Appendix B regression, which clusters based on bank name (autocorrelation check), the $150 billion threshold has the greatest economic and statistical significance. Another adjustment made by the autocorrelation check model is that the G-SIB cap add-on variable becomes statistically insignificant.

**Table 3.1** shows the results of the GLS model using Bloomberg as a credit control variable and exploring a range of alternative variables, including G-SIB and asset size, meant to proxy for a too-big-to-fail effect.

| Dependent Variable: Markit 5y CDS | Baseline Specification | G-SIB (0,1) | G-SIB (cap addon) | Assets Continuous | Assets > $50 B | Assets > $100 B | Assets > $125 B | Assets > $150 B | Assets > $200 B | Assets > $250 B |
|---|---|---|---|---|---|---|---|---|---|---|
| Bloomberg 5y est CDS spd | 0.874*** | 0.879*** | 0.874*** | 0.875*** | 0.878*** | 0.869*** | 0.850*** | 0.842*** | 0.856*** | 0.858*** |
|  | -0.00869 | -0.00881 | -0.00889 | -0.0088 | -0.00861 | -0.00868 | -0.00865 | -0.00853 | -0.00851 | -0.00846 |
| G-SIB (0,1) |  | -0.152*** |  |  |  |  |  |  |  |  |
|  |  | -0.0239 |  |  |  |  |  |  |  |  |
| G-SIB (cap addon) |  |  | -0.0964*** |  |  |  |  |  |  |  |
|  |  |  | -0.0138 |  |  |  |  |  |  |  |
| Assets Continuous |  |  |  | -1.29e-07*** |  |  |  |  |  |  |
|  |  |  |  | -8.82E-09 |  |  |  |  |  |  |
| Assets > $50 B (0,1) |  |  |  |  | -0.797*** |  |  |  |  |  |
|  |  |  |  |  | -0.0388 |  |  |  |  |  |
| Assets > $100 B (0,1) |  |  |  |  |  | -0.456*** |  |  |  |  |
|  |  |  |  |  |  | -0.0305 |  |  |  |  |
| Assets > $125 B (0,1) |  |  |  |  |  |  | -0.687*** |  |  |  |
|  |  |  |  |  |  |  | -0.0298 |  |  |  |
| Assets > $150 B (0,1) |  |  |  |  |  |  |  | -0.751*** |  |  |
|  |  |  |  |  |  |  |  | -0.0291 |  |  |
| Assets > $200 B (0,1) |  |  |  |  |  |  |  |  | -0.442*** |  |
|  |  |  |  |  |  |  |  |  | -0.0269 |  |
| Assets > $250 B (0,1) |  |  |  |  |  |  |  |  |  | -0.492*** |
|  |  |  |  |  |  |  |  |  |  | -0.0261 |
| Constant | 0.213*** | 0.257*** | 0.275*** | 0.267*** | 0.929*** | 0.525*** | 0.745*** | 0.812*** | 0.453*** | 0.469*** |
|  | -0.0339 | -0.0369 | -0.0364 | -0.0357 | -0.0471 | -0.0421 | -0.0407 | -0.0399 | -0.0372 | -0.0366 |
| Liquidity Fixed Effects | Yes | Yes | Yes | Yes | Yes | Yes | Yes | Yes | Yes | Yes |
| Time Fixed Effects | Yes | Yes | Yes | Yes | Yes | Yes | Yes | Yes | Yes | Yes |
| Geographical Fixed Effects | Yes | Yes | Yes | Yes | Yes | Yes | Yes | Yes | Yes | Yes |
| BIC | 9,087 | 9,028 | 9,048 | 9,008 | 8,991 | 9,032 | 8,818 | 8,740 | 8,887 | 8,846 |
| Observations | 3,002 | 3,002 | 3,002 | 3,002 | 3,002 | 3,002 | 3,002 | 3,002 | 3,002 | 3,002 |
| Number of Banks | 71 | 71 | 71 | 71 | 71 | 71 | 71 | 71 | 71 | 71 |

*** p<0.01, ** p<0.05, * p<0.1

**Table 3.2** shows the results of the GLS model using Bloomberg as a credit control variable and exploring a range of alternative variables meant to proxy for a too-big-to-fail effect, including a clearing bank dummy variable in addition to G-SIB and asset-size variables explored previously.

| Dependent Variable: Markit 5y CDS | Baseline Specification | G-SIB (0,1) | G-SIB (cap addon) | Assets Continuous | Assets > $50 B | Assets > $100 B | Assets > $125 B | Assets > $150 B | Assets > $200 B | Assets > $250 B |
|---|---|---|---|---|---|---|---|---|---|---|
| Bloomberg 5y est CDS spd | 0.874*** | 0.880*** | 0.875*** | 0.875*** | 0.877*** | 0.869*** | 0.851*** | 0.844*** | 0.858*** | 0.859*** |
|  | -0.00871 | -0.00884 | -0.00892 | -0.0088 | -0.00863 | -0.0087 | -0.00868 | -0.00858 | -0.00856 | -0.00851 |
| Clearing Bank | -0.227*** | -0.180*** | -0.157*** | -0.178*** | -0.219*** | -0.226*** | -0.206*** | -0.214*** | -0.207*** | -0.299*** |
|  | -0.0606 | -0.0538 | -0.0693 | -0.072 | -0.0569 | -0.0551 | -0.0463 | -0.0459 | -0.0517 | -0.0601 |
| G-SIB (0,1) |  | -0.118*** |  |  |  |  |  |  |  |  |
|  |  | -0.0249 |  |  |  |  |  |  |  |  |
| G-SIB (cap addon) |  |  | -0.0744*** |  |  |  |  |  |  |  |
|  |  |  | -0.0154 |  |  |  |  |  |  |  |
| Assets Continuous |  |  |  | -1.28e-07*** |  |  |  |  |  |  |
|  |  |  |  | -9.04E-09 |  |  |  |  |  |  |
| Assets > $50 B (0,1) |  |  |  |  | -0.770*** |  |  |  |  |  |
|  |  |  |  |  | -0.0386 |  |  |  |  |  |
| Assets > $100 B (0,1) |  |  |  |  |  | -0.461*** |  |  |  |  |
|  |  |  |  |  |  | -0.0304 |  |  |  |  |
| Assets > $125 B (0,1) |  |  |  |  |  |  | -0.679*** |  |  |  |
|  |  |  |  |  |  |  | -0.0296 |  |  |  |
| Assets > $150 B (0,1) |  |  |  |  |  |  |  | -0.738*** |  |  |
|  |  |  |  |  |  |  |  | -0.029 |  |  |
| Assets > $200 B (0,1) |  |  |  |  |  |  |  |  | -0.435*** |  |
|  |  |  |  |  |  |  |  |  | -0.0272 |  |
| Assets > $250 B (0,1) |  |  |  |  |  |  |  |  |  | -0.499*** |
|  |  |  |  |  |  |  |  |  |  | -0.0265 |
| Constant | 0.288*** | 0.295*** | 0.303*** | 0.312*** | 0.974*** | 0.579*** | 0.779*** | 0.841*** | 0.479*** | 0.519*** |
|  | -0.0363 | -0.0383 | -0.0374 | -0.0373 | -0.0477 | -0.0433 | -0.0415 | -0.0406 | -0.0383 | -0.0378 |
| Liquidity Fixed Effects | Yes | Yes | Yes | Yes | Yes | Yes | Yes | Yes | Yes | Yes |
| Time Fixed Effects | Yes | Yes | Yes | Yes | Yes | Yes | Yes | Yes | Yes | Yes |
| Geographical Fixed Effects | Yes | Yes | Yes | Yes | Yes | Yes | Yes | Yes | Yes | Yes |
| BIC | 9,068 | 9,031 | 9,048 | 8,998 | 8,976 | 9,018 | 8,811 | 8,737 | 8,885 | 8,833 |
| Observations | 3,002 | 3,002 | 3,002 | 3,002 | 3,002 | 3,002 | 3,002 | 3,002 | 3,002 | 3,002 |
| Number of Banks | 71 | 71 | 71 | 71 | 71 | 71 | 71 | 71 | 71 | 71 |

*** p<0.01, ** p<0.05, * p<0.1

## Conclusion

This paper seeks to use the best available credit and liquidity controls to explain a sample of international banks' observed five-year single-name CDS spreads. In this regard, the paper uses both credit and liquidity control variables not previously used in the literature. Even with these more robust controls for credit and liquidity fundamentals, the best fit model still would include asset size as an explanatory variable for banks' observed CDS spreads. If credit fundamentals and liquidity differences are properly controlled for, it is not apparent, aside from a too-big-to-fail effect, why the asset size of a bank would strengthen the model.[12]

The data suggest that models using nonlinear asset-size thresholds have the most economic and statistical significance. Banks perceived as too big to fail, based on asset-size thresholds, have CDS spreads 44 to 80 basis points lower than other banks. The study finds that the econometric models that use asset thresholds of $50 billion to $150 billion to indicate a too-big-to-fail effect have the best fits (both via R-squared in the OLS regressions and BIC in the GLS regressions) and largest too-big-to-fail coefficients (when checked for autocorrelation).

There have been calls from some policymakers to change the $50 billion Dodd-Frank Act threshold. Heightened prudential regulation for large firms presumably seeks, at least in part, to address market failure associated with lack of sufficient market discipline arising from investors' perceptions of too big to fail. This paper offers an analytic contribution on the question of size thresholds for heightened prudential regulation of large banks. We recognize that CDS spreads are but one way of considering this topic – systemic importance data, rating agency ratings uplift, and cross-sectional systemic risk metrics are other possible approaches.

---

[12] We would anticipate economies of scale to be "priced in" to the equity valuation of large banks and captured in the credit model used in that paper, as well as in the credit model used in this paper's analysis.

# References

Ahmed, Javed and Anderson, Christopher and Zarutskie, Rebecca, Are Borrowing Costs of Large Financial Firms Unusual?, accessed from SSRN on September 30, 2014.

Bassett, W. 2014. Using insured deposits to refine estimates of the large bank funding advantage. Federal Reserve Board working paper.

Bisias, D., Flood, M., Lo, A., and Valavanis, S. A Survey of Systemic Risk Analytics, OFR working paper, January 2012.

Bloomberg Credit Risk DRSK, Framework, Methodology and Usage, accessed November 2014.

Demirguc-Kunt, A., Huizinga, H., 2013. Are banks too-big-to-fail or too-big-to-save? Journal of Banking and Finance 37, pg 875-894.

GAO, U.S., 2014. Evidence from the bond market on banks' "too-big-to-fail" subsidy. GAO 14-621, United States Government Accountability Office Report to Congress.

Markit CDS Liquidity User Guide 2014, accessed through the internal OCC Economics database.

Jacewitz, S., Pogach, J., 2012. Deposit rate advantages at the largest banks. Working paper available at SSRN.

OFR Brief "Systemic Importance Indicators for 33 U.S. Bank Holding Companies: An Overview of Recent Data." February 2015.

Santos, J, 2014. Evidence from the bond market on banks' "too-big-to-fail" subsidy. Economic Policy Review.

Volz, S, Wedow, M, Market discipline and too-big-to fail in the CDS market: Does banks' size reduce market discipline? Journal of Empirical Finance, Volume 18, Issue 2, March 2011, pg. 195-210.

**Appendix A.**
Autocorrelation Check: Robust Regression Clustered by Bank Name

| Dependent Variable: **Markit Five-year CDS** | Baseline specification | Bloomberg | Moody's |
|---|---|---|---|
| Bloomberg five-year estimated CDS spread | | 0.879*** | |
| | | -0.011 | |
| Moody's Credit Edge five-year estimated CDS spread | | | 0.963*** |
| | | | -0.157 |
| Constant | 0.335*** | 0.313** | -0.348 |
| | -0.422 | -0.240 | -0.369 |
| | | | |
| Liquidity Fixed Effects | No | No | Yes |
| Time Fixed Effects | Yes | No | Yes |
| Geographical Fixed Effects | No | No | Yes |
| | | | |
| Observations | 1,475 | 1,475 | 1,475 |
| R-squared | 0.170 | 0.918 | 0.696 |

*** p<0.01, ** p<0.05, * p<0.1

# Appendix B.
## Autocorrelation Check: Robust Regression Clustered by Bank Name

| Dependent Variable: Markit 5y CDS | Baseline Specification | G-SIB (0,1) | G-SIB (cap addon) | Assets Continuous | Assets > $50 B | Assets > $100 B | Assets > $125 B | Assets > $150 B | Assets > $200 B | Assets > $250 B |
|---|---|---|---|---|---|---|---|---|---|---|
| Bloomberg 5y est CDS spd | 0.895*** | 0.883*** | 0.886*** | 0.881*** | 0.896*** | 0.887*** | 0.873*** | 0.856*** | 0.864*** | 0.860*** |
| | -0.024 | -0.0242 | -0.0238 | -0.024 | -0.0236 | -0.0268 | -0.031 | -0.0281 | -0.026 | -0.0249 |
| Clearing Bank | -0.527 | -0.253 | -0.313 | -0.426 | -0.476 | -0.468 | -0.373 | -0.322 | -0.315 | -0.443 |
| | -0.377 | -0.365 | -0.415 | -0.417 | -0.359 | -0.358 | -0.323 | -0.319 | -0.299 | -0.284 |
| G-SIB (0,1) | | -0.366* | | | | | | | | |
| | | -0.198 | | | | | | | | |
| G-SIB (cap addon) | | | -0.183 | | | | | | | |
| | | | -0.111 | | | | | | | |
| Assets Continuous | | | | -2.27e-07*** | | | | | | |
| | | | | -8.05E-08 | | | | | | |
| Assets > $50 B (0,1) | | | | | -0.852*** | | | | | |
| | | | | | -0.226 | | | | | |
| Assets > $100 B (0,1) | | | | | | -0.413** | | | | |
| | | | | | | -0.185 | | | | |
| Assets > $125 B (0,1) | | | | | | | -0.774*** | | | |
| | | | | | | | -0.264 | | | |
| Assets > $150 B (0,1) | | | | | | | | -0.858*** | | |
| | | | | | | | | -0.254 | | |
| Assets > $200 B (0,1) | | | | | | | | | -0.627*** | |
| | | | | | | | | | -0.211 | |
| Assets > $250 B (0,1) | | | | | | | | | | -0.700*** |
| | | | | | | | | | | -0.206 |
| Constant | 0.446** | 0.466** | 0.448** | 0.470** | 1.140*** | 0.748*** | 0.961*** | 0.993*** | 0.680*** | 0.703*** |
| | -0.214 | -0.22 | -0.217 | -0.212 | -0.276 | -0.201 | -0.292 | -0.28 | -0.244 | -0.24 |
| | | | | | | | | | | |
| Liquidity Fixed Effects | Yes | Yes | Yes | Yes | Yes | No | Yes | No | No | No |
| Time Fixed Effects | Yes | Yes | Yes | Yes | Yes | Yes | Yes | Yes | Yes | Yes |
| Geographical Fixed Effects | Yes | Yes | Yes | Yes | Yes | Yes | Yes | Yes | Yes | Yes |
| | | | | | | | | | | |
| R-Squared | 0.86 | 0.86 | 0.86 | 0.87 | 0.87 | 0.86 | 0.87 | 0.88 | 0.87 | 0.87 |
| Observations | 3,002 | 3,002 | 3,002 | 3,002 | 3,002 | 3,002 | 3,002 | 3,002 | 3,002 | 3,002 |
| Number of Banks | 71 | 71 | 71 | 71 | 71 | 71 | 71 | 71 | 71 | 71 |

*** $p<0.01$, ** $p<0.05$, * $p<0.1$